MARRIAGE:
BUILDING DREAMS THAT COME TRUE

By Bob Groeneman

MARRIAGE:
BUILDING DREAMS THAT COME TRUE

By Bob Groeneman
bgroeneman@rez.org

Copyright © 2016

ISBN-13:
978-0997008609 (Robert Groeneman)

ISBN-10:
0997008601

Unless otherwise indicated, all Scripture quotations
are taken from the New International Version of the
Bible.

To Tammie.
Many times we marvel at how God uses us and we say to each other "We're just a couple of goofballs!" but, I know we are really just talking about me because you are precious beyond words.

TABLE OF CONTENTS

Preface   6

Forward   7

Introduction   9

Chapter 1. The Vision   13

Chapter 2. The Lot   17

Chapter 3. The Soil   23

Chapter 4. The Builder   27

Chapter 5. The Fence   31

Chapter 6. The Curb Appeal   37

Chapter 7. The Infestation   41

Chapter 8. The Neighbor   49

Chapter 9. The Housewarming   55

Chapter 10. The Garage   63

Chapter 11. The Timeline   67

Chapter 12. The Legacy   75

PREFACE

"There goes a lord who tamed a wild shieldmaiden of the North."

-Lady Eowyn speaking of what people would say of Faramir taking her as his wife.

Early in our marriage my wife Tammie would jokingly challenge me with this line from J.R.R. Tolkien's classic book *The Return of the King*. "Wild shieldmaiden of the north" was not a far off description of my beautiful young bride's spicy and wild personality. But, did I have any business even trying to tame her? The constant challenge to protect, lead and encourage her brilliant yet sometimes impetuous creativity is what has endeared her to me in the deepest way after 36 years of our adventure together. I hope that the following notes from our lifetime journey might bring you insight and be a blessing to your marriage.

-Bob Groeneman

PS. I was going to call this book "How to Tame your Wife" but Tammie wouldn't let me.

FOREWORD

From my sons when I taught this message at the Resurrection Fellowship Men's Advance:

Traditionally thought to be the worst position of ministry, a battle field where young pastors pay their dues and prove themselves: Jr High youth groups are the boneyard of Christian service. Experts insist that pastors should stay in this position no more than 3 years, lest they burn out in a fiery burst. Yet there is one creature who scurries across this landscape with dexterity and ease.

Pastor Bob Groeneman has not just survived this harsh landscape, he built his home there. Soon, a culture sprung up around him, growing with incredible speed. Like a magnet, this culture attracts, combines, and unites people into family - and has been doing this for over 30 years. It's the ministry that Pastor Jonathan said could "rule the world."

What you will hear in this session is promised to be logical, applicable, and foundational. Listen to every word closely, because one of them will contain the key to your identity as leader of your family.

Please welcome the expert of analogy. The key master. Our father: Pastor Bob Groeneman.

Sincerely: Dustin, Fletcher & Parker Groeneman.

INTRODUCTION

As a Youth Pastor for 25 years I discovered that the message students need to hear is very much influenced by the position in which they find themselves. The kids I meet who have grown up in the church have heard the message of the love of God so completely and thoroughly that many actually lose the fear of God. Their attitude can be "Sure, I know God loves me, now let's go party." They may even realize they will feel guilty for their sin but they know they will always have God's unconditional forgiveness available to them.

The message a good youth pastor will share with kids in this condition is from Isaiah 6:5 *"Woe to me!" I cried. "I am ruined! For I am a man of unclean lips, and I live among a people of unclean lips, and my eyes have seen the King, the LORD Almighty."*

Isaiah, the good church boy, needed an encounter with the presence of God to strike him with such power that it ruined and unraveled him. Without such a power encounter the casual treatment of God leaves many church kids living very carnal lives.

While Isaiah's message is critical for church kids it would never be the message you would present to a lost, beaten person who has never known love. Indeed if an unloved person walked into a sermon that was describing the severe and awesome power of God it may further drive him from the gospel.

I realize the same situation is true for teaching on marriage and women in general. The culture in which I grew up women were exploring all manner of independence in their families and careers.

When I began to follow God in earnest it was easy to understand the truth that women were qualified to minister in the church. Paul addresses women as co-workers in Philippians 4:3 and Colossians 4:15; they were clearly serving the Lord to the benefit of the whole church. I still believe that women are an important part of leading the church. But, the point of correction that turned my marriage into a great blessing was the startling realization that I had a role as a husband. Tammie's role as my wife was different (yet in many ways much more important) than what I was called to be. I had been abandoning my responsibility to lead, carry, protect, and care for my family and Tammie in particular. I finally submitted to God's role as husband much like a soldier submits to orders to enter the front lines of battle. I could have lived comfortably having my independent minded wife carry the burden, but she was not made for it; the load was killing her and we both knew it. We began to let God show us how our different strengths could fit together.

A woman who has suffered a lifetime of demeaning manipulation, which indeed is a widespread problem, can understandably be offended by the same truth that set my wife and I free. If this is your situation you may want to give special attention to the section titled "What headship is not."

May God bless you as you follow his blueprint for building your marriage.

CHAPTER ONE: THE VISION

BUILDING YOUR CASTLE

*You have just found the blueprints to build something
amazing. As you unroll the mysterious scroll you notice
it's been written on ancient yet durable parchment. You
can tell that many people before you have looked at these
plans and many have tossed them aside saying the plans
are unworkable. But as you look, different features begin
to catch your eye. You imagine walking across the front
yard towards the impressive tower, how proud you
would feel if this design became your reality. The plan
has a beautiful kitchen and family room area, you can
almost hear the laughing and fellowship during meals
and major events. The bedroom opens into a beautiful
walled garden. It becomes easy for you to imagine
romantic escapades in this beautiful secluded area. You
look away from the plans for a moment and wonder if
building this kingdom is really worth all the effort. You
begin to reach for a nearby catalog of prefabricated
houses that offer a cheaper, simpler approach, the people*

in these pictures sure seem happy. There is even a "move in special" that requires no paperwork.

You pause and begin to recall the happiest couples you have ever known. They were always the risk takers, venturing to build their lives with a larger than life pattern. Their lives were always a comfortable yet wonderful place to visit. Your fondest memories were the times visiting these people's castles. Their impressive grounds always seemed to possess undiscovered marvels and unlimited adventure. Just as you consider all of this something extraordinary on the parchment catches your eye. Looking closer you can hardly believe what you see: It's a stamp in the lowest corner "These plans were prepared exclusively for..." your name has been carefully inscribed inside this box. At that point you decide that no matter what the cost, no matter what the effort these are the plans you will follow to build your house.

WHAT IS MARRIAGE?

So, what is a husband and wife anyway? What do these roles mean and and what does each do? Let me state right off that the culture we live in will not help us with the answers to these questions! Today's

American culture has such a lousy track record with marriage that it's time we question everything our society endorses in this regard. Imagine a house builder who loudly claims that everyone should buy his product, while he publicly mocks the houses built by his competition. Yet, half of this arrogant builder's houses collapse while people are living in them. Now imagine these wounded people again buy from this "expert" and 60-70% of the houses again collapse. The loss of life would be catastrophic and people would rightfully question this experts building practices. With our culture's current understanding of marriage this is exactly the devastation taking place. Fifty percent of first time marriages fail along with 60-70% of second attempts. Perhaps we need to rethink our ideas and allow some humility to make us teachable on this subject. Advice on how a husband builds a happy life with his wife, and how she finds freedom to thrive, can not come from our own opinions or from the world but instead is found in the human race's original owner's manual: the Bible.

SOMEONE'S BRIGHT IDEA VS. WHAT REALLY WORKS

When a young man or woman gets serious about building a family they must know what they are looking for. Public opinion may have duped us into believing that marriage is nothing more than getting a co-ed roommate with sexual benefits. If this is indeed the goal then hook up with someone that is good looking, tidy, will pay their own way and will not bother you too much. Certainly don't complicate the issue with legal paperwork. The problem is the human heart cannot be satisfied with such a superficial arrangement and begins to long for something much deeper in the relationship. That "something more" is not provided and arguments arise because more is hungered for than what was originally promised. Often this type of relationship is abandoned causing any emotional roots that have begun to grow even in this shallow relationship to be ripped out of the living souls involved and a wounding collapse brings down the house.

With new eyes let us study these original and proven blueprints and in the following pages look at God's amazing plan for a thriving marriage.

CHAPTER TWO: THE LOT

BUYING THE LOT
With plans in hand you set out to find the perfect lot to fit your dream. You know that what you build must be a perfect fit to the size and shape of the property.

ARE ROLES RELEVANT TO MY LIFE?

Right off it becomes obvious that the Bible's description of a husband and wife often reads like a job description. And indeed it does because God understands that those seeking marriage are actually seeking to fill a role. It would be strange for someone who wanted to be a part of a wonderful fairy tale to refuse to enter the story as one of the characters. Yet people who enter marriage with worldly thinking do exactly that.

People can be offended at the Bible's description of marriage because it outlines roles for the participants. There are some people who would react negatively to the obligation of any role (except perhaps King of the

World) because they feel like a role primarily indicates restrictions. But, let me state that we should not be offended at being given a role. Just like in any working organization, if we are to fit together in relationship with others it is the acceptance of a role that makes it possible.

We need to consider the great benefit offered by certain roles even if they contain specific limitations. The benefits can far outweigh the restrictions. Think of the benefit afforded by the vastly different roles of a lock and key when they work together. When you use a lock and key to secure your treasure chest the lock goes on the box and the key goes in your pocket. When the two pieces are true to their design the entire mechanism is a great success. We would never ask "which one is greater or more important?" How useless the device would become if the lock complained that the key gets to travel the world while it is stuck on a box. And also if the key lamented that instead of being attached to a beautiful treasure it had to live in a dark pocket. Each becomes tempted to forfeit their unique role and in turn, forfeit the treasure that belongs to them both! Which item, the lock or the key, is better? The question itself is irrelevant. Let us not participate in the madness of believing any role in a marriage is better or worse just because it is different. Each man and each woman is best suited to the position God designed for them.

THE GREAT HUMILIATION

Some people may consider their position under God significant but refuse to see any importance in the way they are positioned with other people. In Luke 14:8 Jesus warned of a great humiliation some people will suffer when they misjudge or ignore the authority of others in their life. *When someone invites you to a wedding feast, do not take the place of honor, for a person more distinguished than you may have been invited. If so the host who invited both of you will come and say to you, "Give this man your seat" then **humiliated** you will have to take the least important place.* Placing yourself out of correct order with other people is an absolute disgrace in the kingdom of God. The people at this banquet were each sitting in correct order. Their placement corresponded to a knowledge of who should sit above them and who should sit below them. The host made no interference until someone arrived who thought these distinctions were of no importance and simply chose the chair to his liking. To this person the host brought a humiliating correction. It is to our own shame that we ignore our roles and proper position with others. This is an area of our life that God wants us to give careful attention.

THE HUSBAND'S ROLE

So what are the husband and wife's prescribed roles? Fasten your seatbelts because the New Testament in 1 Corinthians 11:3 is going to offend every bit of worldly advice you ever swallowed. *Now I want you to realize that the head of every man is Christ, and the **head of the woman is man**, and the head of Christ is God.* Without tiptoeing around what the Bible clearly describes as foundational, and without apologizing for what the Bible states as essential, the simple truth for a happy marriage begins here: The husband's role is the head of the marriage. (See also Eph 5:24)

Why would the Bible promote such an unfair and suffocating tyranny? This arrangement may on the surface seem horrible and demeaning but as a couple begins to cooperate with their assigned functions something quite wonderful begins to happen. Rather than living as two individuals with one of them in charge, a functioning unity is formed; all the pieces fit in place and a treasure is unlocked. Frustration vanishes as the God-orchestrated roles work to bring mutual fulfillment. I ask again that you set aside any prejudice you may have concerning God's word on marriage and instead honestly consider how these roles might work in your own life. You will begin to see how God makes all things amazing.

CHAPTER THREE: THE SOIL

PREPARING THE GROUND

You are unsure, at first, how to prepare the ground for building, you know that the land must be made ready to accommodate the structures. Suddenly you notice, printed right on the plans, notes detailing what the condition of the ground must be.

WHERE DO I START?

This arrangement found in 1 Corinthians 11:3 can be likened to an algebra equation that makes sense only when both sides match. The verse says *Now I want you to realize that the head of every man is Christ, and the head of the woman is man, and the head of Christ is God.* And the first part of the equation looks like this: The head of man is Christ=The head of the woman is man. The truth of man being the head of the woman works in equality with the truth of Christ being the head of the man. You could try to emphasize the point of the man to woman relationship and ignore the man to Christ relationship, but nothing in your marriage will add up. The first and most important thing a man can do to improve his marriage is to lose his pride and earnestly seek God. Any man who sits around thinking the first step to improving his marriage is to get his wife to change gets a big fat "F minus" in marriage math. To prove this look at the last phrase of this verse which is another part of the equation: *"the head of Christ is God."* A man waiting around for a correct response from his wife before he aligns himself to Christ is as ridiculous as Jesus waiting around for a correct response from us before he aligns himself to the Father.

Jesus moves first in obedience to God and through his obedience we are won to him. The same will be true for you and your wife; husbands must be willing to take the first step. Repent, learn, serve and lay down your life even if your wife does nothing. This is Jesus' example to us.

IS THE WOMAN INFERIOR?

1 Corinthians 11:3 says *The head of the woman is man.* And so some will ask "does this mean the woman is inferior?" But look, this verse goes on to say *The head of Christ is God.* So the same question can also be asked "is Jesus inferior?" The answer to both is no. This arrangement of roles in no way implies that one is

inferior to the other. We can see this truth as we look at what the Bible says about Jesus in John 1:1. This verse makes it clear that Jesus is absolutely equal to God: *In the beginning was the Word, and the Word was with God, and the Word was God.*

But in 1 Corinthians 15:27-28 we see that Jesus is also subordinate to the Father *For He "Has put everything under His feet." Now when it says that "everything" has been put under him, it is clear that this does not include God himself, who put everything under Christ. When he has done this, then the **Son himself will be made subject** to him who put everything under him, so that God may be all in all.* Since Jesus himself accepts a subordinate position we have to conclude that this role cannot also mean "inferior." Functioning in a subordinate role never requires us to devalue our worth. Even though the employee is under his boss's authority no one thinks the boss is more valuable as a human being. A subordinate role never indicates inferiority. We must stop confusing these very different things.

"SUBMIT TO ONE ANOTHER OUT OF REVERENCE FOR CHRIST"

Ephesians 5:21 says *"Submit to one another out of reverence for Christ."* Now, whatever Ephesians 5:21 is teaching us, we know that it certainly is not telling us that the structure of the roles in the marriage should be ignored. Let's look at these 4 verses from Ephesians 5:21-24 together. *"Submit to one another out of reverence for Christ. Wives, submit to your husbands as to the Lord. For the husband is the head of the wife as Christ is the head of the church, his body, of which he is the Savior. Now as the church submits to Christ, so also wives should submit to their husbands in everything."* After stating that we should submit to one another Paul continues with three strong statements emphasizing the roles of marriage. We are admonished to submit to one another, but as clearly stated, the roles we live in must not be abandoned. In the same way, no one would expect a father, who strives to lovingly serve the desires of his children, to abandon his role as provider by making his small children equal managers of the family's financial obligations. A good father maintains his role as provider while submitting himself to serve the needs of his children. And so we can see what is meant in this mutual submission: even as a wife submits to her husband the husband will always submit to serving, protecting and providing for his wife, putting her needs above his own.

CHAPTER FOUR:
THE BUILDER

YOU HAVE TO BE THE GENERAL CONTRACTOR
When you see the scope of the work you begin to wonder if it wouldn't be easier to simply hire a builder to take over the project. After several conversations with potential builders you realize no one has the same vision that you do for the project. Some of these builders suggested bringing in prefab modulars for many of the features you described. All of them want to cut back extensively in the design of the foundations you know are needed. If this is going to turn out right you decide you will have to build it yourself.

THE HUSBAND'S INFLUENCE

Something to notice in the verse from 1 Corinthians 11:3 is the word realize. *Now I want you to* **realize** *that the head of every man is Christ, and the head of the woman is man, and the head of Christ is God.* To realize is to become aware of a fact that already exists rather than to make something happen. Headship of the husband is a fact, not a command. Sometimes men think "Yes I know, the bible says I **ought** to be the head." No sir, you **are** the head. Striving with your wife about who leads the marriage is simply proof that you don't yet believe this fact. A man's attitudes, actions and words are, in fact, steering his family and printing a brand on them whether he knows it or not. Whether a man is forceful and strong or timid and withdrawn he is placing a character over his wife and kids that influences their lives.

Imagine in 1885 the now famous cola giant decides they are not going to associate their product with any brand because they believe it might make a negative impression. So, instead they handwrite the product name in pencil every time it is used. The unavoidable result is that today the brand on the product would be it's name handwritten with pencil. Therefore even a man who abandons his family with the thinking "I will leave so I am not a bad influence" is actually branding his wife "Absent Husband" and branding his kids "Absent Father." Thinking your influence has no weight is a misperception. The wife and kids may respond by taking charge and filling the leadership vacuum. The result is an appearance of strength, but the branding of "absent authority" remains as an unseen foundational effect for the rest of their lives.

Sir, please realize that you are the head. You are, right now, branding the identity over your wife and your kids, good or bad, whether you like it or not. Wishing it were not so does not change this fact.

THE HUSBAND'S DUTY

As husbands, how are we supposed to manage this terrifying responsibility? The answer is in our prime duty prescribed in Ephesians 5:25. *Husbands, love your wives, just as Christ loved the church and gave himself up for her.* We may think that *"Just as Christ loved the church"* means I have to love my wife really, really, really lots! This isn't far wrong, but there are details that will give us the specifics of what this means. Jesus' love is defined in this verse with the action that he *"gave himself up for her."* Husbands, you already know what *"giving yourself up for her"* means because right before you got your girl to say "I do" you gave her the distinct impression that she was the center of your life. By all appearances, every decision that you were making, or would ever make, would be to serve her and for her benefit all because of your great love for her. In this you were *"giving yourself up for her"* and becoming to her what Christ is to the church. Many husbands drift away from this devotion and wonder why their wife feels abandoned. You will act in

Christ's character and you will reclaim the magic of those first years together if you will go back to that first love and give yourself to her again.

CHAPTER FIVE: THE FENCE

BUILDING THE FENCE ON YOUR PROPERTY LINE

One of the projects you are now busy with is building a fence on your property between your house and the neighbor. Your neighbor approaches you with some concerns. Many of the changes you are making on your property are not to his liking. One thing he insists is that you move the fence, he even offers to help you build it in a different space. Besides that, he says the style of fence you have chosen is completely unacceptable. Being a good neighbor is important to you so you think about it for a few days. After reviewing the plans you become aware that the fence as shown on the plans is critical to the working of the overall layout. You choose to do what must be done and build your fence even though your neighbor greatly disapproves. Time passes and your castle is becoming majestic and beautiful. Years later this same neighbor approaches you humbly and says he now sees the wisdom of the way you laid out your fence and living spaces. He desperately asks you for help building his own boundary lines around his family.

TAKING FULL RESPONSIBILITY

This brings us to another detail of what our love must be if it is to be *"how Christ loved the Church."* Jesus' love included taking responsibility for all the sin of all the people. It can be a big shock for some men to realize that as husband they must assume this level of responsibility for their wife. Yet it is this level of covering and protection the wife must experience to fully thrive.

This level of headship can be easily seen in other areas of life. For example, if your dog bit someone you would be responsible for the incident even though it was not your teeth biting the mailman's ankle. Everyone agrees that you are not personally guilty yet you would still have to respond to any citations and pay any fines. Again, if your employees broke the law you as the head of the corporation would have to manage the consequences. You would be responsible even though you are not guilty. All this makes so much sense until God asks us to be the head of the marriage and we can't seem to believe that He is asking us to be responsible for all the family problems. Some men run great businesses yet when it comes to their family suddenly they are hands off. To refuse responsibility for your wife is to reject your role as husband.

OWNERSHIP

Whether we are talking about husbands, fathers or even pastors the Bible describes an ingredient that is often missing in leadership: ownership. In our families we must be much more than a detached observer acting as an occasional teacher or referee. John 10:12 makes it clear that we need the heart of the owner. *The hired hand is not the shepherd who **owns** the sheep. So when he sees the wolf coming, he abandons the sheep and runs away.* The message in this verse is clear; the man who refuses to own the sheep does not have the heart of God.

Years ago I was leading our youth service and was complaining to God "I wish these kids would enter into your presence Lord, will you teach them to worship?" God replied to me "If they had a Pastor then he would lead them into worship!" That statement shocked me because I called myself their Pastor. I began to rethink my responsibility. I started to take ownership of the spiritual condition of my youth group. Here is the question I had to ask myself: do I have the attitude of a hired hand or do I have the heart of the owner? The owner takes full responsibility while the hired hand says "They don't pay me enough to deal with these problems."

The same thing is true for your family. If something has been given to you then you must own it. Think about your home, you wish it was a peaceful, fun and love-filled environment, instead of a strife-filled scream factory. Think about your kids, you wish they would make the right choices but instead you say "Sure he's only 10 but I can't control what he does." Think about your wife, you know her high pressure job is killing her because you see the physical complications and headaches but you say "I let my wife do what she wants. **It's not my deal.**"

The word husbandman refers to a person who cultivates the land; a farmer. Think for a minute what the land looks like without the farmer. Imagine a man who has taken no responsibility for his parcel of land, it is a mess of weeds and broken buildings. Imagine this same man walks by a farm that has been kept beautiful, trim and abundantly fruitful and says "This farmer just lucked out, he doesn't have to deal with weeds and broken equipment like I do." This statement reveals the man's profound ignorance. Likewise for husbands, the first step of victory is to accept the fact that the condition of your family is what you have let it become. **It is your deal!**

Accepting ownership is not just a good idea, the Bible makes it clear in Matthew 25:20-26 that refusing to take ownership is wickedness. Two of the men in this story brought their master double the talents they had been given. Five had been turned to ten and two had been turned to four. To both men the master replied, *"Well done, good and faithful servant! You have been faithful with a few things; I will put you in charge of many things. Come and share your master's happiness!"* When the one-talent-guy comes along, please listen to what his excuse is. *"I knew that you are a hard man, harvesting where you have not sown and gathering where you have not scattered seed. So I was afraid and went out and hid **your** talent in the ground. See, **here is what belongs to you.**"*

This man's entire argument: "I don't own this" did not work well with the Master. The servant reasoned "This money is not my deal, I barely even touched it." He hoped it would get him off the hook. Instead it brought the response *"You **wicked, lazy** servant!"* We cannot simply walk away from the things we have been given. Imagine saying to God on judgement day

"Here's these wife and kids. They are a mess but it's not my fault, I barely touched them." What do you expect to hear from the Master?

In Song of Songs 4:12 the wife is compared to a locked garden. An enclosed garden speaks of protected beauty and fruit reserved exclusively for the owner. But, it is only the husbandman who can maintain this wall of protection. The negligent husband will allow the wall to fall into disrepair which will let the world walk in, steal the fruit and destroy the beauty of the garden. The diligent husband will tend, protect and watch over his wife because he knows that he is responsible. *I went past the field of the sluggard, past the vineyard of the man who lacks judgment; thorns had come up everywhere, the ground was covered with weeds, and the stone wall was in ruins.* (Proverbs 24:30-31)

CHAPTER SIX:
THE CURB APPEAL

JOB OFFERS FROM PEOPLE WHO SEE WHAT YOU ARE BUILDING

Your project is well under way. Many of the features you once only dreamed about are starting to appear. As the months go by, you begin to get offers from area businesses asking you to join them. The strengths they see you building on your property are the same things they want in their company. Your options continue to increase and become more and more profitable.

YOUR MARRIAGE AND SERVING GOD

Let me make you aware that the way a man leads his family is the key for anything he wants to do for God's church. 1 Timothy 3:4-5 is very clear about this. *He must manage his own family well and see that his children obey him with proper respect. (If anyone does not know how to manage his own family, how can he take care of God's church?)* When a young man wants to be in the ministry he should work on his resume. What is his resume? It is his family. Therefore his best progress is made by taking a wife and starting a family.

The reason a family reveals someone's ministry qualifications is that every principle a person needs to lead the church is already being practiced by a man whose wife and children are thriving. When a man knows what is required in the role of husband and does those things, he experiences an amazing assistance from heaven, along with tremendous personal fulfillment. At the same time his wife and kids experience freedom, protection and emotional peace. What happens in a healthy family needs to happen in a healthy church; this is how we build God's Kingdom.

RESULTS CAN NEVER BE 100% GUARANTEED

Let me also say that when a man assumes his proper role as husband and father and takes full responsibility for the lives of his family, the result of "perfect lives" cannot be 100% guaranteed. Although health, beauty and emotional well-being should be the expected result of godly leadership, people's free will is still involved. Jesus gives us the example of how godly leadership can still fail to produce a positive result. Jesus had twelve disciples, who each experienced an environment of perfect leadership yet one chose to walk away from his place. We cannot judge another man's failed marriage or wayward child any more than we can say that Jesus should have done a better job discipling Judas. Then again, don't let Judas be your excuse for leaving a path of broken lives behind you. For a man who doesn't shrink from his responsibility as husband, father or pastor, these lost and broken lives will be the exception rather than the rule. To those that experience the exception: do not lose heart. God has made a promise to work things out for you. Even in the face of disappointment and pain, He is faithful.

CHAPTER SEVEN:
THE INFESTATION

THE LAWYER'S VISIT

One day a lawyer visits as you are building and says he wants to help you. He has noticed that your wife isn't doing her fair share of the heavy lifting. He suggests a few appropriate citations that might snap her into shape, all perfectly legal mind you. You are at first caught off guard by his words, you never thought of it this way before. You begin to feel an anger growing in your heart as you consider the unfair expectations of single handedly building this estate. For days you are tormented with the unfairness of your assignment until finally, you go get the plans to tear them up. Losing this once beautiful dream is more than you can stand but you just can't allow your wife to continue to take advantage of you. It is through tears that you notice the stamp in the corner once again. Underneath where your name has been written was something you hadn't seen before "To whoever is faithful to this project, I will be faithful to you." Then, clearly written, is the personal signature of the master designer himself. You realize this promise was made personally and directly to you. You see that the success, or failure, of this mansion will depend upon the commitment of just one person: you. You deeply repent, horrified at yourself for how close you came to throwing the whole dream away. You quickly find the lawyer and remove him from your property vowing to never again listen to his logic.

SHE ISN'T DOING ANY OF THE HEAVY LIFTING

One of the things that husbands stumble over are the times when they feel like they are required to carry an unfair portion of the family responsibilities. This bitter root takes hold with the mistaken idea that the marriage contract is primarily between them and their spouse. Men often quit on marriage because they fail to remember that the covenant with their wife is only secondary; it is fundamentally a covenant with God. At what point did you begin to believe this cute young girl you married had the ability to deliver into your hands a portion of God's Kingdom? If a husband ever feels slighted or overworked by his family obligations he needs to do business with the Lord who gave him the promises.

Are God's terms not to your liking: you give yourself and your feeble efforts to love and care for a woman and in return God hands you a beautiful kingdom so similar to his own heaven that you can not help but be humbled by his generosity? This dynasty you inherit is so much more than you deserve. Your contribution seems a miserable pittance in comparison. Men, do not be tricked into giving up such a great reward: keep working, keep building.

THE OL' BALL AND CHAIN

Some men admit that they have abandoned the command to give themselves up for their wife because they feel like they are faced with a choice of either being tied to "The ol' Ball & Chain" or moving forward in their "God given destiny to change the world." They summarize their predicament as a choice to serve their wife or serve God. What is God's answer for a man who finds himself in this dilemma?

The answer can be seen when we look at the man who knew the presence of God better than any of us and who was in charge of a world changing ministry to establish God's Kingdom on the Earth. I am talking about the first man Adam. Adam was commissioned to *"fill the earth and subdue it."* (Genesis 1:28) Then a horrible choice was presented to him in Genesis 3:6 *"She also gave some to her husband, who was with her."* In that moment Adam was faced with the prospect of joining his wife in her broken condition thereby abandoning the highest calling ever given to a man. Adam chose to be with his wife even though it cost him everything. It was from this position of togetherness that God made a way to redeem them both. I believe this is a choice every person faces, at some level, in marriage. It is only by making the choice to cling to your wife that God can bring his plan of full salvation to both of you.

Of course, a like minded wife can let her husband go away for seasons of effective ministry, but a man who moves away from his vows because he wants to serve God, rather than serve his wife, is doing something that should not be done. Your wedding day was your decision to join her. When you are married, choosing your wife over every other thing becomes your highest calling. Paul describes husbands as putting the needs of their wives first in 1 Corinthians 7:32-33 *An unmarried man is concerned about the Lord's affairs--how he can please the Lord. But a married man is concerned about the affairs of this world--how he can please his wife.* Paul doesn't label this distraction as "sin" instead he refers to it as what is expected. No matter what noble achievement a man thinks he is stepping into, if it involves abandoning his wife, it is the path of the ungodly. 1 Timothy 5:8 says it this way: *If anyone does not provide for his relatives, and **especially for his immediate family**, he has denied the faith and is worse than an unbeliever.*

THE MAN IS THE DRIVER

My favorite illustration of how a happy marriage works is a family taking a road trip. The man is in the driver's seat and he has asked a girl to join him. She has agreed and so she becomes his wife and sits in the passenger seat. From her position she has the ability to study maps and ponder the condition of the landscape. The wife has information that the driver does not have; she can give insight and has a God given intuition about their journey. A wise husband will depend on this information before reaching any decision. She may tell him "The kids are tired and we need to stop. The map says that the next exit has a restaurant and gas station." Why any man would ignore his wife's insight and advice is one of the greatest mysteries of humanity.

Equally so, the husband has a unique vantage point and can see road hazards the wife will not notice. Also, he will be the one to actually steer the car off the highway which illustrates how the final decision truly lies with him.

Trusting each other is, of course, the basis of this relationship. Trusting another person at this level may seem unwarranted but this trust ultimately comes from our faith in God. We believe that God's hand is on our spouse and, if needed, we believe God has the ability to turn their heart. God's faithfulness causes me to understand that even though He must work through imperfect people and situations God will always fulfill his promises to me.

Sometimes an inexperienced husband can swerve towards the ditch and, because of fear, his wife faces a great temptation to grab the steering wheel and take control. The husband is at first offended but then can settle into a habit of laziness which allows his wife to run the show. The wife is stressed with the responsibility of keeping the car on the road but also enjoys the control. This scenario leads to the most common dysfunction of marriage seen today: the lazy husband and controlling wife. The reason this arrangement is so common is because each response plays to the other's basic sinful tendency.

Let's look at what these basic sinful tendencies are. They are fought by every man and woman since the fall and are described by God in Genesis. The man, having been designed to rule the world and provide for his family, experiences after the fall a new feeling of laziness that works to hold him from that purpose. Genesis 3:17-19 describes two different things that will now work against the man. *To Adam he said, "Because you listened to your wife and ate from the tree about which I commanded you, 'You must not eat of it,' "**Cursed is the ground** because of you; through painful **toil** you will eat of it all the days of your life. It will produce thorns and thistles for you, and you will eat the plants of the field. By the **sweat** of your brow you will eat your food until you return to the ground, since from it you were taken; for dust you are and to dust you will return."*

The first will be the very laws of nature: the earth will not easily cooperate with Man's role as ruler. The other complication is a new attitude of laziness that Adam experiences. I believe "toil" and "sweat" point to this inner reluctance to do what the man was made to do. This inner resistance is laziness, which all men must overcome, and is contrasted by what we read in

Ecclesiastes 5:19 *to accept his lot and be happy in his work--this is a **gift of God***. It takes a supernatural grace from God for men to enjoy work because our natural sinful tendency is to resist our obligations.

The woman who was designed to use all of her amazing abilities to help her husband rule the world also experiences a sinful drive that keeps her from that purpose: control. God speaks to her about a new sin element that will influence her life in Genesis 3:16 *"And you will desire to control your husband, but he will rule over you."* (New Living Translation) For a wife with a lazy husband the temptation to control is admittedly overwhelming. However, driving from the passenger's seat, while doable, is incredibly taxing. A woman who trusts God with her life, and then lets go of the steering wheel of their marriage, does two things. She gives herself the freedom to be the best navigator possible and also gives her husband the chance to learn godly leadership, since no one can learn to drive while someone else is steering.

CHAPTER EIGHT:
THE NEIGHBOR

YOUR NEIGHBOR'S ADVICE

Months later another neighbor comes for a visit.

"Understand yer tryn' to build a purdy cabin and keep yer woman in line?"

You just look at your feet and don't know how to answer. "Well, sort of." you offer.

"Take it from me pal, you gotta show these women folk who's boss right from the get go. Lay down the law. Like me, I got my wife shingling the shed for the past two days. She's still not so good at it though, seems like the hammer slips out of her hand everytime I check up on her. Durn near hit me in the head a couple times."

"Thanks for the advice." You say wishing he would just go away.

"Listen, this is my fourth wife, so I know what I'm talkin' bout. I make her a nice chore list ever' day and if she doesn't finish it I "accidently-on-purpose" break one

of her favorite heirloom dishes at dinner that night.
That teaches her a good lesson."
You can't believe what you are hearing. Finally he starts
to leave but turns to say one last thing "Well, if you need
any more marriage advice just come n' give me a holler."
He's finally gone and you head inside to tell your wife
how much you love her. You wonder how much longer
this hillbilly genius will be able to keep wife number
four.

THE MOST IMPORTANT CHAPTER: WHAT HEADSHIP IS NOT.

HEADSHIP IS NOT CONTROL.

One of the most important details when we talk about headship is talking about what headship is not: Headship is not control! Think of Jesus role in your life. He takes full responsibility while still giving complete freedom. God will never micromanage your life because he is committed to the most important principle of love: free will! The husband must do likewise. You must be the wall that protects your wife, but inside the garden your wife (the tree) has unlimited freedom to grow. In this relationship the wife can be smarter and have more talent than the husband and it does not change his role to provide for and protect her. If you are not providing your wife a sense of profound freedom then you are not husbanding well. You are to set your wife up as the reigning queen in a beautiful kingdom you have built exclusively for her. By God's strength working in you, every need is provided, every question answered and she is protected from every danger.

HEADSHIP IS NOT MANIPULATION.

Manipulation is when you use anything **except** your positional authority to get your way. Manipulation is most commonly used because someone wants something that is outside their authority. They scheme, campaign and fight until they get what they want. It is a wicked art that some people are quite good at. They are often only thwarted when they encounter someone who stands unmoving in their proper authority. If you understand this principle you understand the basis for victory in spiritual warfare. More on that in my book about authority.

However, the type of manipulation I want to highlight here is used by people who have a position of leadership but do not have the personal courage to properly exercise their authority. Husbands and fathers can fall into this group. King Ahab in 1 Kings chapter 21 is history's poster child for cowardly leadership. Even though he had the position of king, manipulation became the hallmark of his kingdom. His wife Jezebel came in and asked him, *"Why are you so sullen? Why won't you eat?"* He answered her, *"Because I said to Naboth the Jezreelite, 'Sell me your vineyard' But he said, 'I will not give you my vineyard.'"* *Jezebel his wife said, "Is this how you act as king over Israel? Get up and eat! Cheer up. I'll get you the vineyard of Naboth the Jezreelite."* If Ahab would have had the courage to stand in his positional authority as king of the land then he could have made the arrangements necessary to move forward in his final decision on the matter. Instead he allowed his wife's scheming manipulations to run rampant in his kingdom. Jezebel hired scoundrels to slander Naboth; then they killed him. *When Ahab heard that Naboth was dead, he got up and went down to take possession of Naboth's vineyard. (verse 16)* Take a minute to mentally assess who the responsible person is for this innocent man's murder. In verses 17-19 we see who God holds responsible. *Then the word of the LORD came to Elijah "Go down to meet Ahab. Say to him, 'the LORD says: Have* **you not murdered a man** *and seized his property?'* God blamed Ahab for the manipulative situation that led to this murder. And so we see that whatever we allow to happen in areas under our authority is our fault. When Jezebel indulged her lust for control and King Ahab sat around playing the immature and lazy coward, the result was that Ahab was guilty of murder.

The weak leader will partner with any available "boogey man" who will inflict painful consequences on situations he doesn't like. Either that, or he will bring indirect pain that cannot be traced directly to himself. "Oh look, I told you not to leave your bicycle in the driveway and I 'accidently' ran over it." This is the coward's way.

HOW DOES YOUR LEADERSHIP STYLE AFFECT THOSE AROUND YOU?

Imagine the bitterness, unanswered questions and cruel sense of life being out-of-control that Naboth's family and friends were forced to navigate. The lawlessness that manipulation releases into your kingdom is the atmosphere of hell and every evil work functions in this state of confusion (see James 3:16.) The weak leader does not reinforce the understanding of authority but rather teaches those around him that the most effective manipulator can win the day. We must renounce manipulation in all it's forms and choose to lead with courage.

A direct decision, even if highly unpopular, makes it possible for people to accommodate the situation. If King Ahab would have made the decision, that was within his authority, to annex the property around his palace, giving generous compensation to all those affected, of course Naboth would have hated it, but he could have recovered and moved on with his life. Consider the simplicity of the strong leader's statement "This is the direction we must go. If you don't like it you need to deal directly with me." Only the courageous leader's approach prepares those around him to learn an even greater truth: we must ultimately submit to and come to terms with God, the highest authority.

CHAPTER NINE:
THE HOUSEWARMING

AS YOU BUILD, YOU KEEP DREAMING

People admire your endurance as you build. Several times friends comment on your faithfulness to your project. But it is not a mystery to you. The same motivation that caused you to start this project keeps you going. Everything you build you do with your wife and family in mind. The back porch addition is done thinking of family parties. The library is built thinking of quiet evenings reading together. The bedroom is remodeled thinking of intimate moments with your beautiful wife. The grounds are kept perfect thinking of how pleased you will both be picnicking in the yard. Everything is formed around these feelings of love and because of that, nothing seems hard. Why anyone would abandon such a beautiful life seems more and more of a mystery to you.

WORSHIP AS A PICTURE OF THE STRENGTH OF MARRIAGE

All growth in our marriage relationships comes from an attentiveness to our wives that has all the characteristics of our worship towards God. All our attention and affection are focused on the one we love and this becomes the basis of our relationship. When problems with money or sex become distractions to intimacy sometimes couples begin to ignore their love relationship and focus on the problems. This is the same tendency we have as believers to focus on our sin. But, I hope you have learned in your spiritual life this approach doesn't work and is, in fact, a distraction from the real answer which is a heart focused on Jesus. The strength to overcome sin comes from inside our close relationship with God, not from our effort against the problem itself. If you as a husband struggle with porn you will not find the strength to fully overcome with a direct attack against the lust itself. The victory is to reawaken affection and renew the chase for your wife. You must see, once again, in your bride everything you ever desired. Cling to her, make her again the center of your attention and all your energy. Remember this is how you lived when you were first dating and first married. During those early years you amazed yourself that porn had literally disappeared from your life. The problem now is that you have been distracted by the turmoil of the battle. In your spiritual life and in your marriage, go back to the principle of pure worship and your first love.

In worship we instruct people to forget everything else and just experience the presence of God. Do not stand in a worship service thinking about your sin, instead let it be covered by Jesus' forgiving sacrifice on the cross. Realize that God doesn't use times where we draw near to him as the avenue to bring our sin to our attention because, for God, intimacy is the goal. So a couple should not use every close moment to bring up and work through problems. The worship and the closeness is actually the answer to all other things.

I want to present to you the fact that your connection to your wife and your connection to God are virtually inseparable. 1 Peter 3:7 shows us that our prayers can only pass through a marriage filled with respect. *Husbands, in the same way be considerate as you live with your wives, and treat them with respect as the weaker partner and as heirs with you of the gracious gift of life, **so that nothing will hinder your prayers**.* In fact, your relationship with God and with your wife is so intertwined that you won't be able to distinguish them when you are talking about either one. Paul spends 11 verses in Ephesians 5 talking about the relationship of marriage and then concludes in verse 32 *This is a profound mystery--but I am talking about Christ and the church.* Every principle of closeness, affection and loving with all your strength applies to both. Of course a man should never place his wife above God but according to Paul's pattern in Ephesians 5 a good husband will be able to talk on and on about how much he loves his wife and somewhere along the line everything runs together until he finally says "Oh by the way, I am also talking about how much I love Jesus." This deep, rich and supernatural love from God eventually overflows and blends into every other relationship you have; it begins most profoundly with your spouse.

WHY YOUR WIFE IS MAD AT YOU

I am about to break the communication code in your marriage and promote you to the rank of the honored King of your castle. Those arguments you fall into with your wife that seem like insanity are all based on the fact that you forgot who you are. A man will often say "People at work understand me fine, but somehow my wife just doesn't get it!" Let me help you understand something: you are not in a business relationship with your wife. This connection with her is unlike any other relationship you have. What must constantly be reaffirmed is the fact that you are daily choosing to be her husband. When your wife says "I'm overextended and vulnerable." What must she hear from you? Any doctor, neighbor or random magazine article can tell your wife "Hey, just learn to be a team player." But, **only a husband** can reply "I will protect you."

When your wife says "I've been rejected." Any friend can tell her "Just don't listen to them, their opinion doesn't matter." But, **only a husband** can say what she needs to hear: "You belong to me."

Let's say you send your sad, lonely wife to visit the specialist. You know she needs a strong sense of identity to snap her out of her depression and give her daily routine purpose. How do you expect her to discover her identity? There is only one man with whom she shares the same name. If this man does not make it clear that she belongs to him then she begins to feel like she doesn't belong at all. If the wife's core identity come from sources outside her husband it weakens the very marriage foundations you have been hoping to build. Of course enriching and healthy relationships outside the marriage can flourish but nothing can ever come close to the influence the husband holds. No doctor's visit can cure a back-peddling husband who is abandoning his marriage vows. Perhaps some men hope that the pill their wife takes will numb the fact that they are failing as a husband?

When your wife says "I'm hurt." and you answer "You'll be fine." instead of "I will carry you." it is no mystery why she responds from a painful emptiness claiming that you refuse to help her. You told this woman, in fact you promised, that you would be her husband, her covering. But now you position yourself like a common bystander. The husband who has accepted his place as the responsible head will continually communicate these things: "You belong to me." "I will protect you." "I will carry you."

YOU CAN HELP YOUR WIFE BE BEAUTIFUL

The bible actually connects Sarah's physical looks to her relationship to her husband in 1 Peter 3:5-6 *For this is the way the holy women of the past who put their hope in God used to make themselves beautiful. They were submissive to their own husbands, like Sarah, who obeyed Abraham and called him her master.* We know Sara's beauty was not just "beauty within" because the very natural eyes of the Egyptians saw something besides a great personality. *When Abram came to Egypt, the Egyptians saw that she was a very beautiful woman.* (Genesis 12:14) Could this attitude of Sarah's heart have actually been the thing that affected her looks? Could the unseen actually have an effect in the physical realm? Of course! Remember, this is what Christians believe about all of life, duh! The spiritual realm is preeminent and what is true spiritually is the pattern for what we see in the physical.

First, you can help your wife keep her beautiful attitude and looks by being less of a jerk. Plus, while you are working on that, you must continually call her beautiful, let your words wash over her and transform her. You will be married to the most enviable beauty in Egypt. Others may want to take her but she won't leave you because she knows that you are the vital channel of what makes her stunning!

CHAPTER TEN: THE GARAGE

LIVING IN THE GARAGE

You go visit a good friend. He has been working long hours building his house and is beginning to get very weary of his whole project. He tells you that going to dinner at night is such a hassle that it's easier for him to just spend the night in his garage rather than sort through all the family issues. You try to remind him why he started building in the first place but he says it's too late, the feelings are all gone. As you head back home you are thankful for the passion you have been careful to keep alive for your wife over the years. You decide it's time to take that second honeymoon.

YOUR SEX LIFE

Many men cannot seem to own their sex life. Instead of leading their wife into greater sexual freedom and fulfillment they try every trick they can think of to get what they want in bed. They don't have the personal character to develop a satisfying sex life in their marriage without resorting to manipulation. They are not mature enough to patiently lead without giving up. Because of this many men slip into an angry and manipulating attitude where they find themselves "accidentally on purpose" letting their heart become adulterous and then they blame their wife for their sin.

How you lead your wife's body is part of your marriage responsibilities because pure and honorable sex is an important part of your spiritual life. God has this crazy idea about our sex life that is explained in 1 Corinthians 7:5. *Do not deprive each other except by mutual consent and for a time, so that you may devote yourselves to prayer. Then come together again so that* **Satan** *will not tempt you because of your lack of self-control.* This verse makes it clear that there are times we come together with our wives in sex and it puts a restriction on Satan's activity. So, we can conclude that there are some important situations in our married life that don't need more prayer, they need more sex. Men, don't be lazy in this area of your life. Since sex inside a marriage has the ability to limit Satan's power then please realize that your sexual drive running outside your marriage will release Satan's power against you. Sex is a powerful part of building a strong marriage but it can also destroy you. Keep it inside your fence and it will remain an important and positive weapon in your spiritual life.

TO HAVE AND TO HOLD

Another aspect of your physical relationship with your wife is emphasized in one of my favorite phrases of the wedding ceremony: "Do you take this woman to be your wife, to love and to cherish, **to have and to hold** as long as you both shall live?" At this point the guy says "I do" and all the girls sigh. We have all noticed that when a new couple falls in love all they ever do is hold hands, hug and kiss. Anything to touch each other. Compare that to an angry couple who comes in for counseling saying "We haven't had sex in many months." It's already quite clear that the man stopped touching his wife long before. Here is a good rule for every man: never stop touching your wife. How? The way you did when you were dating. First, you never forced yourself on her; that approach only leads to face slaps and restraining orders. Instead you chased her to win her like the Bible describes in Genesis 2:24 *Therefore shall a man leave his father and his mother, and shall cleave unto his wife: and they shall be one flesh.* Cleave means to catch through a continual pursuit! You found ways to sit close, hold her hand and put your arm around her. Never stop doing that. Charm her, woo her, win her, touch her and always hold her.

CHAPTER ELEVEN:
THE TIMELINE

UNDER CONTRACT

You can't help but think back to the days immediately before the purchase of this property. The promise of what the house would be was such a big dream that you wondered many times if it would really come true. One time when you were feeling extra lazy you suggested to your girl that you both just go and live on the lot and maybe you could put up a tent or something. She hated the idea and you argued with her about her stupid stubbornness. Days later you apologized to her as you realized it wasn't what you really wanted either. That was the day you once again committed yourself to follow the plan as designed by the master. The payoff for doing it the right way has been unbelievable, just look around at this beautiful estate you own.

HONOR HER CONSCIENCE SEXUALLY

While we are talking about physical contact let me stress that the man should never urge his girl to violate her conscience in premarital sex **especially** if he intends to marry her. If you do not intend to marry her then let me be the first to say what a giant loser you are to urge her to give away all her assets for nothing in return. But for the man who intends to live many happy years with this girl please realize you are effectively teaching her that she doesn't have to follow her conscience in sexual matters. Some men put themselves in a position where all their effort and convincing ends up working against their sex life after they are married. After the wedding when she has the feeling "Don't touch me," this foolish boy has trained her to ignore her conscience when it comes to 1 Corinthians 7:4 *The wife's body does not belong to her alone but also to her husband.* Sure that's what God says but remember, you taught her to ignore God's direction. Here is the better pattern to live by: we honor God's principles **before** the wedding and we honor God's principles **after** the wedding.

Husbands love to celebrate 1 Corinthians 7:4 where it says his wife's body belongs to him, because "Hey, that sounds like a lot of fun." But before you shout "glory," be sure to read the rest of the verse. *In the same way, the husband's body does not belong to him alone but also to his wife.* Your wife has ownership over your body as well. This doesn't translate to playing doctor the same way it does in the guy's brain. Her concern will be to keep you healthy and it is her right to tell you what to eat. Her opinion about how you look and what you wear is also her business. If you want access to her body then you must take seriously your wife's access to your physical issues. Only good things can come of it.

UNREALISTIC EXPECTATIONS

Men and women can both approach marriage with unrealistic expectations. Boys thinking girls exist that do not have strong feminine drives and girls thinking boys exist that don't have strong masculine drives are both common fantasies.

The culture can feed the lazy man an expectation that he can have a lifetime of sex without all the effort that a courtship, commitment, wedding and family supporting career would require. Porn supports the fantasy that girls exists who don't act with any feminine drive. Indeed, a girl who is driven by the lust for sexual pleasure and disinterested in the commitment of a secure relationship is acting like a man. Boys who feed on porn are moving away from the ability to fall in love with and appreciate what a woman really is. Unless he breaks this illusion, a man will be trapped in recurring superficial relationships, looking for something that does not exist in reality. Some men may even be tempted to join the gay sex lifestyle because it's easier than the work of accommodating what seems to be a woman's complicated emotional needs.

Women can also develop unrealistic sexual expectations and the culture is happy to feed their fantasy. The woman's fantasy is not as culturally offensive or as easily identified as the man's fantasy expressed through porn. Sometimes the woman's misconceptions can actually be encouraged by the church. The commonly held illusion is this: good men are not motivated with a strong desire to have sex. Let me state clearly that very few men have the gift of being a eunuch. In fact, being free from the motives of sexual passion is described by Paul in 1 Corinthians 7:7 as a special gift rather than a man's normal condition. *I wish that all men were as I am. But each man has his own gift from God; one has this gift, another has that.*

Then in 1 Corinthians 7:9 we are shown that in regard to his sex life a man has but two choices. *But if they cannot control themselves, they should marry, for it is better to marry than to burn with passion.* One choice is to marry and have sex, the only other choice is to have a gift from God where you do not burn with passion. So the vast majority of young boys, since they don't have this gift, must be taught how to honorably channel their sexual energy. They should be taught to expect that as they are patient and careful to plan their marriage then they can have what they wanted all along: lots of sex. This is much more constructive than continually making them feel guilty for having normal feelings. When sin is not carefully distinguished from the normal sexual appetite and the entire mix is condemned as wickedness it causes many driven young champions to renounce their number one motivator. Let's stop doing this!

Often the first reaction of a guilty young man who has let his passion lead him into sin is to wish away his sex drive. This becomes a vow against the very desires which would motivate him to build a family and help resolve his dilemma. Let us instead recommit ourselves to the good fight of keeping this strong sexual current in its proper channels. Before they were married I told my own sons "A godly girl wants a motivated and faithful young man to build a life with, and a godly boy wants to get down her pants honorably." The response I got from my boys was "OK. Now that's something I can work towards!"

The way the culture feeds unrealistic expectations to girls is to present the image of men who are focused, centered and devoted to a woman with no sexual motivation. Girls, if you want to find a man who is motivated to make your marriage exciting and full of passion then do not marry a boy that has no sexual energy. Such a boy would be called a "eunuch."

There was a recent, popular book (written by a woman) where one of the main boy characters would crawl into bed and cuddle, comfort and hold the distressed heroine all night long. In the book this happened dozens of times and this fictional boy character was not once aroused or motivated sexually. (There is no "hunger" in this boy's "game".) The only way such a scenario is possible is that the boy is, in reality, a eunuch! Self control is not being displayed just because a boy has somehow lost his God-given arousal mechanism; self control is displayed when a boy refuses to enter a situation with a high sexual context. Finding himself unmoved after making such a poor and dangerous decision is most unnatural.

In the name of speaking the God honoring truth, I must report to you girls that virtually every good church boy is still preoccupied with sex. The only ones you will find to argue this statement will be the boys' mothers. Isn't it curious that the fathers never protest this point? If the boy is also smart (in addition to being good) then he will have thought about boundaries in his sexual life. I want to emphasize that a boy puts these boundaries in place because he is good, not because he is bad.

Girls can play dangerously close to a boy's boundaries not realizing the great risk. Of course the boy's foolish actions are ultimately his own responsibility but if things progress the girl ends up giving away her most powerful assets without the boy committing any of his. The girl is always taking the biggest risk in any premarital sex scenario. The best boys, however, are trying to figure out how to win the girl while honoring the will and ways of God. If girls will stay with God's plan for sex inside marriage they will get a lovely chase, romantic love story, a nice home and a devoted man.

CHAPTER TWELVE:
THE LEGACY

MOVE IN DAY

Your own son has grown up and has caught the wonderful excitement of what he has seen you build over the years. He has dreamed of building his own mansion and has chosen to do things under the brilliant advice of the master builder. He has also sought your counsel often and has now arrived at his own "move in day." This is the most exciting day of his life and because everything has been done with honor and respect all the family and friends are able to enjoy this celebration with him. You as his father are filled with overwhelming joy. You know that he is beginning the greatest journey any man can undertake.

THE CEREMONY

There are many principles of the husband and wife relationship summarized in the wedding ceremony. Let me point out just a few of these.

One of the best principles is illustrated in the act of the father bringing the bride down the aisle and giving her to the groom. This is significant because a girl is protected under the authority of her father until the time she is given in marriage and into the protection of her new husband. Girls are given in marriage. Boys on the other hand, leave their father and mother and are united to their wife. (Matthew 19:5) In other words boys take a wife, while girls are given in marriage.

In the ceremony much is made of the miracle of joining; it cannot be simply undone without great damage to all involved. The unity candle is an amazing picture of two lives becoming one; the couple's identities actually become blended. At the beginning of the ceremony the mothers light two candles each representing their child. After the pronouncement of husband and wife the couple uses these candles to light the central candle and, in a symbol of giving up their personal identity and committing themselves to the identity of the marriage, they blow out their individual flame. Sure the moms cry but it is very precious.
We also ask for the intentional agreement of the congregation emphasizing God's will in the union.

Many elements of the traditional ceremony have deep meaning but people still choose to do things differently. One couple I know had a unity peanut butter and jelly sandwich. He put peanut butter on his bread, she put jelly on her's, they put it all together and ate it. You may need to have a longer time of special music planned for this one.

Feel free to use or change this included ceremony however you wish.

A CEREMONY OF MARRIAGE

First, _____ & _____ want to
thank all of their Family and friends for being a part
of this amazing day and for doing everything that
helped to make this happen.

All of us here will have the privilege of witnessing
God's best come to pass in the lives of this wonderful
couple.

Who gives this woman to be married to this man?
(Her mother and I)

_____ take your bride and step forward.
Please remain standing as we pray.

Jesus let your love and presence be so real here today.
Full of your life and joy. Mark this event with your
glory.

You may be seated.

CHARGE TO THE BRIDE AND GROOM

As I read from Ephesians 5, I want you to realize that
these are the words that God is going to honor in your
lives today. The world has the idea that marriage is, in
essence, a legal contract but we know it is much more
than that: it is a spiritual bond. It is the miracle of a
spiritual union.

From Ephesians 5 it says: *Wives submit to your husbands as to the Lord. For the husband is the head of the wife as Christ is the head of the church, his body, of which he is the Savior. Now as the church submits to Christ, so also wives should submit to their husbands in everything. Husbands, love your wives, just as Christ loved the church and gave himself up for her to make her holy, cleansing her by the washing with water through the word, and to present her to himself as a radiant church, without stain or wrinkle or any other blemish, but holy and blameless. In this same way, husbands ought to love their wives as their own bodies. He who loves his wife loves himself. After all, no one ever hated his own body, but he feeds and cares for it, just as Christ does the church for we are members of his body. For this reason a man will leave his father and mother and be united to his wife, and the two will become one flesh. This is a profound mystery--but I am talking about Christ and the church.*

When we understand the way Jesus is joined to His Church then we will understand the miracle of the marriage relationship. Your lives are joined together and you become one. The same power that joined you to Jesus when you made him your Lord will join the two of you together. Do not question this miracle. This union that is happening between you today goes beyond your feelings.

Consider this illustration: if I woke up and my arm was asleep and had no feeling & I didn't feel close to it anymore; it would still be critical that I remembered two important things: 1. These feelings do not accurately reflect the unity I still have with my arm. The feeling itself is misleading. And 2. The consequences would be tragic if the feelings were acted upon and I divorced or cut my arm from myself.

What is happening between you today is a joining miracle, and it is a precious and permanent thing.

To the friends and all the witnesses here let me say this:

You are not here just because of tradition. You are here to be a witness forever to this miraculous union, and to add your agreement before God to what is taking place. Don't ever tamper with this miracle. From this day forward, regardless of what comes, you are in agreement with this union. Don't doubt it, don't speak against it or attempt in any way to cause it to be anything other than a happy union.

_____ & _____ have each heard God's voice and have full confidence that this union is the perfect will of God. They have followed Jesus to this beautiful moment. So, for all of us, we commit ourselves to them, until the end of this age, to do everything in our power to see that this union remains solid, strong, happy and prosperous. Let no one tamper with it or cause it to be anything other than the perfect and beautiful love story that God has planned.

This is a miraculous thing, and it is of God

PROFESSION OF VOWS: TO GROOM

_____, do you take _____, as your wife, as your own flesh, to love her even as Christ loves the church, to lay your life down for her, to protect her and care for her, to have and to hold, for the rest of your lives? (I do.)

Then turn to her and say

I _____/ according to the word of God/ leave my father and my mother/ and I join myself to you/ to be a husband to you/ From this moment forward/ we shall be one.

TO BRIDE

_____, do you take _____ as your husband, submitting your life to him as unto the Lord, showing respect to him as the head of this union for the rest of your lives? (I do.)

Then turn to him and say:

I, _____/ according to the Word of God/ give myself to you/ to be a wife to you./ From this moment forward/ we shall be one.

PRESENTATION OF RINGS

May I have the rings, please.

There are countless rings in the world, you each sorted through the choices and came up with the special one and now only these two have been chosen for this moment. All other rings are common, but these are, to you both, holy.

Your lives for each other are the same way. The feeling that the love between you is unique in all the world is from God. THIS love, between the two of you, is a love that is not common. No one has ever experienced it before. It was made only for the two of you. And so, you will wear these rings as a constant reminder of today's unique miracle. Because these rings will be to you the other's love, life and heart.

TO GROOM _____ here is the Bride's ring. This ring is a token of your love and commitment to _____. It is a never ending circle that indicated the unlimited love that only comes from God. This love will always display that you are willing to lay your whole life down for her. This love cannot think in an independent or self centered way. You will find that you never talk or think in terms of "I" From now on everything is "WE" Everything is the two of you together.

_____ you have made it clear to _____ that she is the center of your life and of every decision. Never stop doing that! Year after happy year continue to show her that kind of love. Let this ring be to her your vow that you belong to her. Body and Soul you will protect her and love her.

_____, take this ring, place it on her finger, and say to her:

With this ring/ I thee wed./ It is a token of my love for you/ and a token of my life/ that I give to you now/ in Jesus' Name.

TO BRIDE _____, here is the Groom's ring. Since the beginning the desire of every woman has been to find a place of joy; a protected place of purpose and fulfillment. And I have some great news for you today! This place exists! You will find this out as you continue this story that's beginning today. As you follow God's plan you will enjoy the real sense that you have been placed like a princess in a beautiful, protective, expansive castle; made just for you by your prince charming! Your joy will overflow as you delight yourself in the business and the people of the realm you have been given. Your beauty and grace will increase and you will be admired by everyone who knows you. _____, this love story is not just a dream it is real: God is it's author and it's details are in the Bible. It comes true for everyone who believes it! But sadly many don't believe it, the world is full of their heartbreaking stories. They reject God's pattern for the role of husband and wife, they forfeit the fairy tale and choose the world's idea for marriage that ends all too often in disillusionment. But your lives will not follow the pattern of this world! Instead you will be conformed to the image of Christ, to the pattern of His bride. This marriage will follow that story line.

_____ stay as close as you can to _____. He can't succeed without your wisdom and uncanny intuition. Be the best navigator you can possibly be; full of compassion and insight. Speaking joy about every possibility that is around each corner. That kind of teamwork can never fail.

Let this ring be your vow of this kind of devotion to him.

_____, take this ring, place it on his finger, and say to him:

With this ring/ I thee wed./ I give it as a token of my love for you/ and a token of my life/ that I give to you now/ in Jesus name.

PRONOUNCEMENT

Hold each other please. Let's pray. "Jesus knit them together right now. Let their lives be linked. Let them abandon themselves to one another. Let them find a whole new identity in this union. Work your miracle of joining right now in Jesus name, Amen."

As a representative of Jesus Christ, before Almighty God and in the Name of the Father, of His Son Jesus, and by the power of the Holy Spirit, I now pronounce you one together. You are now husband and wife.

The first thing that _____ and _____ will do as husband and wife is to take communion. Then their family will join them for prayer.

SPECIAL MUSIC:
COMMUNION, UNITY CANDLE, FAMILY PRAYER

BLESSING OF THE UNION

Galatians, chapter 3 says that through Christ the blessing of Abraham will come on the believers, so that we will be those who inherit God's promises. First Peter, Chapter 3, says a man and his wife will inherit together the grace of life. And so, I am going to read to you your blessings and inheritance. This is what you can expect your life to be filled with, so listen carefully.

This is paraphrased from Deuteronomy chapter 28. You will be blessed if you live downtown and you will be blessed if you live in the country. Your children will be blessed and you will raise them and protect them with joy and wisdom. Whatever you create with your hands will multiply and bring great blessings into your life. Your grocery cart, cupboards and refrigerator will be blessed. You will be blessed when you come in and blessed when you go out. Any enemies that would rise up against you will be confounded and defeated. They may come at you from one direction but they will flee from you scattered and confused. The Lord will send a blessing on your checkbook and savings and on everything you put your hands to. The Lord your God will bless you in whatever position he puts you in. The Lord will establish you as his holy, special people; He has promised you this with an oath. These blessings are a gift that you can never earn or deserve. They will find you and overtake you. God will be faithful to you. Then all the people around you will see that you are favored of the Lord, and they will marvel at God's blessings that are on your life and so they will regard you both with respect. The Lord will grant you abundant prosperity; He will open on you the very treasure rooms of his abundance. He will send grace on your lives (always at just the right time) to bless all the work of your hands. You will give generously out of your abundance and will need to borrow from no one. The Lord will make you the first, not the last. Make it your joy to pay attention to the voice of the Lord your God and happily follow His direction. In doing this you will always be at the forefront and you will never be neglected.

These are God's blessings for your new life together.

_____ your blessings are about to begin. You may kiss the bride!

PRESENTATION TO THE CONGREGATION

Please turn and face your family and friends..

Ladies and gentlemen, I present to you Mr. and Mrs.

_____.

ALL EXIT & LAST ANNOUNCEMENTS

GENERAL ORDER OF SERVICE:

Music, Moms light 2 candles and sit

Groom & Preacher enter

Attendants enter and Bride enters

CEREMONY

Wedding party exits

Announcements & People are dismissed by rows

(Don't forget to sign the license.)

www.ingramcontent.com/pod-product-compliance
Lightning Source LLC
Chambersburg PA
CBHW060516280326
41933CB00014B/2989